flipped eye publishing

overrun by wild boars

simple words, rendered sublime

overrun by wild boars

flipped eye publishing
www.flippedeye.net

First published by flipped eye publishing © 2021
Copyright © 2021, Maia Elsner

Cover Concept & Finishing © flipped eye publishing, 2017, 2021
Cover Letter Typeface Design & Front Layout © D237, 2017 | www.d237.com

A huge thank you to the editors of the following journals, in which previous versions of poems in this collection appeared: *Blackbox Manifold, Brittle Star, Coffee House Poetry, Colorado Review, Dust, Magma, Pigeonholes, Poetry Ireland, The Maine Review, The Missouri Review* and *Tinderbox*. Thank you also to those other journals that have supported and promoted my writing.

I am very grateful to Nii Ayikwei Parkes and Nathalie Teitler for including 'On not-translating Neruda', 'Polish honey cake' and 'Transnational Zoo' in *Un Nuevo Sol: British LatinX Writers* (flipped eye, 2019); to Amy Acre and Jake Wild Hall for including 'Christmas in diaspora' in *Field Notes on Survival* (Bad Betty Press, 2020); to Helen Eastman and the Live Canon team for including 'Elegy to the howler monkeys' in *Live Canon 2020 Anthology* (Live Canon, 2020); to Aaron Kent for including an early version of 'For my mother' (published as 'Goldfinch') in *Crossing Lines: An Anthology of Immigrant Poetry* (Broken Sleep Books, 2021). Thank you for the opportunity to be a part of these projects, for the beautiful books you have created, which have allowed me to come into contact with so many writers I admire.

ISBN: 978-1-905233-71-7

LOTTERY FUNDED

Supported using public funding by
ARTS COUNCIL ENGLAND

overrun by wild boars

overrun by wild boars

Contents

as long as paper lasts

echo of constellations

no te juro
eterno amor,
pero ¿no tiene
cada instante
de amor
su propia
eternidad?

Marianne Frenk

the price of tenderness

Cochineal wings

i.

Today I'm four and go to market
  with my mother. She buys lilies

for the imaginary pool I colour in,
  cuts grapefruit peel

into boats, unzips the coat
  of each segment & lays them down –

naked bodies on floating rafts.
  Waxy limbs protect us

from sinking. How skin survives
  a boat ride.

ii.

Tonight I read about Monarch butterflies
  flying south each year –

3,000 miles from Canada
  to Mexico, from milkweed

to wildflower. Not one completes
  the journey. America is full of gossamer

carcasses, flitting between falling
        bullets. There is nothing of butterfly

in my mother. I stop believing
        in symbols.

iii.

Lately I'm concerned by wings.
        A week after my grandmother

dies, I dream
        her head emerges from my own

womb, ashen, except its lips, on which
        a tattooed starling is fixed

in cochineal. Insect wings ground up
        for paste. Later, I begin EMDR

treatment. I am cold as a fish memory
        of the time it takes to cross the Atlantic

twice & end up right where I started,
        with a woman yelling, *go back*

to where you come from –
        her words purpling the dusk.

For my mother

Orange juice pressed fresh in memory,
      this morning, tarter –
      not quite the sweetenough

of home. This early hour, you wonder
      what the hummingbird says
      to the heron of its

migration. Now, the church is sinking
      through the torn-up streets
      of Coyoacan, tree-roots

displacing concrete, bury deep. At dusk,
      the jacaranda scent infiltrates
      colonial walks, cobbles

delineate peripheries & what you were
      slips out unbidden
      with passing years

of you still up at 4am, still jetlagged
      from your first flight,
      when just outside, a bird begins

with me still wondering what part of you
      I lose each day to another
      language, another song.

On finding the painted walls of Bonampak

Underneath the stone temple
my therapist denies me

a glass of water. She says
you are not trying hard enough, dig

deeper. I say something
about the hyper sexualization

of breasts.

                    *

We are in the war room
& there is red

& limbs & limbs & my juddering
fingertips. Outside,

howler monkeys shred the giant
ceiba leaves, suck out

their life-blood.

                    *

After I am attacked, I discover
electric jolts

in skin, sharp
tinging. Later,

a woman hugs me:
if you are this upset at a random assault,

you should get help.

*

I take art history classes. At the RA
Picasso Exhibition, stare

at torn up nudes, body
stretched & split. Is this

what he wanted to do
to them? I get anxious

when my boyfriend touches me.

*

I learn conservation theory.
Remove lime-scale, fill up

cracks. I cannot restore
enough. In the night, I am back

in the war room, shuddering.
Dig deeper as walls

collapse.

Elegy to the howler monkeys

Their shrieks stab the heart of the undergrowth.
My cousin calls me *changita*, little monkey,
chucks me up, his branch arms sprawled, as I hang
upside down. I leap from tree to tree, his friends
welcoming me in. Sharp embrace. I am only fifteen
in the dark when you find me, toss me, fish & bait.

Later, in the C19th library, I read Fanny Hill is bait
for an old man. Walking to my dorm, undergrowth
of nettles & thorns, no dock leaf: I am stung, fifteen
sores, spread red between my thighs. The monkeys
watch. Berger writes that women & women friends
spectate themselves, aware of being seen. I hang

half-out of the window, wind through my hair. Hang
on till I feel something. A boy sniggers. I take the bait –
start another speech about feminism. My friend
says *the history of sex is a very small undergrowth
of fully consensual encounters.* Usually one monkey
initiates, wants more & the other bears it. At fifteen

I don't say much or anything very well. Fifteen
is a time of miracles I don't remember. I hang
from the boat-sails of my sheets, my cotton monkey
climbing clouds. A pterodactyl's on my wall, bait
for the meteorite I keep from wrecking. Undergrowth
keeps growing. No bridge off the cliff. My friends –

imaginary giraffe & ghost moth. The borders of friend-
ship are contrails of smoke. At dusk, I return to fifteen
& the party. The bonfire burns into the undergrowth:
you were my friend & I trusted you. I hang
my letters on sharp rocks, syllables break & I am bait,
ums & silences. Inevitably, I retreat to theory, monkey

at typewriter. Turn in my coursework. Play monkey
for grown-ups. Talk Marxism. Discuss with friends
the problems with university politics. I am bait
for a polite disagreement. But inside I am still fifteen
& I simmer, obsess over every touch. I am hung
up on detail, wade through the footnote undergrowth

of memory: bait the monkey; follow it to the edge
until the undergrowth thins & there's a clearing of friends.
I am not fifteen. I am the hang-man haunting the bridge.

Reflections of the bumblebee (i)

Monkshood is best
flower

for resting
as rain drip

drips
over there

bergamot, sweet
milkweed

snapdragon
red, red

spider perched
cricket nest

blue-tit
eggs, hello

butterfly.

Return

In preparation
for the Magic Cube

championship, I memorize
precise colour

combinations. I walk
through rooms

to replicate
their order when

blindfolded: the yellow
bar at Thirst where you

inserted your hand
into my pants; the red

lights I blacked out
to; my blue skin.

ii.

Sometimes the order changes.
Sometimes it begins

with my green
top I know you

like. Do you know
that all the jade

of Chichen Itzá
was stolen & when

there was nothing
left, the whole

sacred site, its stone
jaguars,

was bought
for $70. I spend $70

on ASOS, pay more
for the shipping fee.

iii.

At dusk, I retrace
my footsteps. But the skull temple

is not where I left it.
The Sun Stone has become

an altarpiece
& Che Guevara

is on the cross.
Who owns the rainfall

gathered on cobbled streets?
Refracted street lights tear apart

a broken city,
Malinche again

violated, her final
quivers, unheard,

unrecorded–

blue moon. Orange
blossom. White eyes.

remains in the rubble

Seeking origins

Naturally we return to the dump full of icons & figurines
tossed by hands, traces of blood & what will be left of us

when all this is over. Will there still be moss & starlings
on telephone wires, shimmering, will anyone notice?

I find a shattered alabaster head, blue-paste eyes, an amber
amulet in which a fruit fly clatters its skeleton wings, sun

lighting it from behind misused condoms & fallen stars.
I too have shouldered my smallness against constellations.

You stand at the brow of the hill, the empty city shuffling
its half-baked ghosts into pale sunlight. Do you see the red

heron's beak dip in & destroy the smooth surface in rings,
sharp & spiderlike? We cling to the warm of flesh, your head

at my neck, eyelashes shuddering the last of last night's
forgiveness, as day breaks this moment, crude & brilliant.

The Roman sarcophagus is all that's left

Carved Miriam, chin turned up towards her spangled tambourine,
crosses the dead sea, women dancing as coral waves spread,
their escape from Egypt captured in alabaster stone & gypsum red –
will we too survive, our lungs flooded, the indifferent machine?[1]

& will we reach the other side? Now in Roman dress,[2] wet dream
that Rome will be saved. The bloody victors determine the past: say
Miriam stands in for Mary & their assuming Christianity paves the way
unchecked for 'righteous' violence, our relics now in ruin.[3] The regime

buries its secrets.[4] Who will keep our statues? The Heygate Estate down
for millionaire flats.[5] Southwark council signs away the Bodeguita Café,
deprived of customers, all dispersed & only flies feast as queso sweats.

Where is the blue-haired girl sucking tamarind, her mum who frowns
at the stars, the Big Issue seller with cracked cheeks who kisses each day
hello?[6] High-rises groan with new bones & burnt-out silhouettes.

[1]   under the guise of scientific enquiry, Barbasco
is patented by UPenn. Sacred rituals pillaged by turista-
pirates outsourcing trials for progesterone to Puerto Rico;

[2]   forced Boricua women are guinea pigs for birth control
to protect against revolution. No outcry as todas operadas
under the guise of scientific enquiry. Barbasco

[3]   now perpetually US owned: PR population control
marketed internationally as *la revolución feminista.*
Pirates outsource trials for progesterone to Puerto Rico

[4]   & no one cares how the legacy of Jim Crow overflows
prisons, children wrenched from homes. Big pharma
under the guise of scientific enquiry preserves Barbasco

[5]   as progress, code for profit, encouraging overdose.
The penthouse settlers gun for highs, cum for limpias,
while outsourcing trials for progesterone to Puerto Rico.

[6]   They slash her open, force rubber limbs, a bamboo womb,
fallopian tube, with no worry for progeny, fuck her. Pay her
under the guise of scientific enquiry, *charity.* Barbasco
pirates outsource trials for progesterone to Puerto Rico.

Transnational zoo

Hide

She is borrowed by coyotes. They take her nape, her womb, her spine, for bearing. She lengthens, her hide thickens, forms mountain ridges, the cactus fence like bars, her ribs. Soaks dishrags at the watering hole. Stitches each together with cochineal thread into new pathways, capillaries. Now a catfish thrusts through jet quartz. Quicksilver ripples over skin. Its membrane, permeable. A great rusted hook clenching in. Another caught along the bank, thrown back; the water hemmed in. How to feed when no pearl on paved streets. Gold is the sun tearing up an oyster's world, this market for tears. She sells them at street corners: invents context, names. Wonders in what language rain falls on tormented cities. Soon, the figs ripen.

Prey

He fell to the wrath of Xolotl. She, to the corner at Calzada de Tlalpan. There was a sacrifice that day. On the shore are washerwomen. They clean the Big House, its labyrinthine corridors, the exits of the sitting room, the bottle-green kitchen. There are no entrances, no letters, no addresses. Each day brings the renewal of tourist visas. To the border, he tracks them, the sea slipping over stones. They say the moon lost her virginity that night & the sun shred itself against the rocks. She was dragged. Dragged through Juarez, then Zapata, General Anaya; spread out finally at his foot. By Francisco Sosa, she was gutted, her antlers removed, her hide skinned, while he was torn by hairless dogs in Coyoacan square.

Cage

In the Bible, Adam gave each animal its name. Kan. Chakmool. Chapulin. Aak. Aayin. Chuwen. Quetzal. By the time the Summer Institute had come & gone, few words were left uncorrupted. In the Lacandona forest, you hear them still, while Akyantho', god of foreigners, brings his pistol & light skin & Jesus Christ, his son, hangs out with Tuub & Kisin. Some names remain. Some are lost as new translations & new transliterations encode distinction. Preacher & zoologist transcribe secrets, sell off sons. Then the rain comes & daughters are washed away. Deposited on the shore: oil-spill rainbows, bits of shell. Now, the Authorities turn people into birds. Some nests are burned. Some wings are broken.

Pilgrims

Sun sheds itself each night against the bauxite-
heavy mountains, tipped edges of rose-finch wings.
To Khondistan & Tibet, Burma & back, they come –
soldiers turned scientists & venture capitalists: pilgrims
pressing lips to fingertips, eyes glistening like dewdrops.
Then coins chink. Beer cans are bought & buried outside

the brothel, where a drag queen hums a lullaby. Outside,
factories churn & chug, hot steam converting bauxite
to aluminum. The orphan on the corner inhales dewdrops
of smoke. Makes a splint for a sparrow with a broken wing
trained to sing to first class carriages & little king pilgrims
worshipping their own images. Tourists & teachers come

following tangled telephone wires & the cicadas come,
whispering their secrets as air sharpens the outside
of sunrise. Wild boars overrun my mind like pilgrims
on the hunt for purpose, gold. I seek calm as bauxite
will release the water it absorbs. As it flows free, wings
pause their clatter & what is left of fear are dewdrops

falling. I turn over clover-stems in search of dewdrops.
There are not enough to water these streets. The kids come
with prayers, their t-shirts torn, their budding wings
are frail as bones. The false gods are of profit. Outside,
apostles mine the village & the hill, break apart the bauxite
mountain. Some boors are assimilated, become pilgrims

to aggression. Tear up the wood, the trees – pilgrims
losing themselves. Their masters, drunk on dewdrops,
drain the lake, fill it with concrete. They say bauxite
is valueless inside the mountain & so they come
with drills & drill & drill into falling stars. Outside
you & I talk of emptiness, of the beetle you saw, its wings

ripped off. Of taking & how easy it is. Of crushed wings,
crushed limbs. The sliver girl with no home, her pilgrim
feathers. Sometimes I believe in a kind god. Outside
I admit to the boars inside me I suppress. Amid dewdrops,
find my own ferociousness, use knives against myself, come
bleeding. You say another way is possible. That bauxite

is worth nothing outside the mountain. That wings
over bauxite springs are pilgrims also. There will be
dewdrops come Christmas, soft footsteps of snow.

Christmas in diaspora

Our usual Chanukah candles
        on the tree, we remember

Babcia, with her fake
        Costa Rican papers

as she crosses to the Christian quarter
        & for this is granted

entrance. There is room at the inn
        this time, as

the Częstochowa Ghetto's liquidated.

        *

This Christmas:
        do not scream, do not

think of Janek
        his side, unclosing

then, Cecilia's sharp
        breath, ripe & violet

how Babcia found them
        aching, how father carries

his name, my baby brother
       also, *Janekito,* I sing to him,

sleep in heavenly peace.

       *

We shred duck, split wing from breast
       slice liver, roast

in goose fat, serve the head, white eyes
       staring up, the cheeks

of the cod are the softest –
       first to disintegrate

tidings of comfort and joy.

       *

My father up early
       to meditate, I see

his grimace scar
       wet cheeks

gashes at his lids
       I breathe with him

namo tassa Bhagavato arahato sammā

may I be free from suffering.

       *

May I be free from suffering

as the she-boar shudders off
     its hurting & the tiger bite

births new skin –
     but the maize-leaf nativity is missing

its baby Jesus
     as is customary

because it is still night
     in Mexico & in diaspora

my brother gifts me
     an amber hummingbird

trained to sing
     Nahua spirituals

to Spanish gods.

Reflections of the bumblebee (ii)

After
drip, drip

where is
monkshood, where is

bergamot, no
milkweed, no

red, red
hot

concrete
ploughed

field, ploughed
people

where is
spider, no

water.

On not-translating Neruda

Es verdad que el ámbar contiene / las lágrimas de las sirenas? - Pablo Neruda
Is it true that amber contains / the tears of mermaids? - translation by
William O'Daly

before translation
        the reflexive speaks of
intimacy
        palmspressed, a child
finding
        her own fingertips
a sunset
        stumbled on
the years inside
        tomorrow, when
es verdad
        is both question & statement;
the Taxonomer translates
        contiene
as *contains*;
        then, caught up
he overlooks
        a figure passing, gloves
clasped
        clutching fragility
in a glance that tears itself
        in translation, now hard
now cold;

but in Spanish, *con* signifies *with,* as in

contigo en una noche estrellada

contigo hasta la luz del día se suicida

bajo una ola morada

enamorada

he misses

the difference

between *contains* and *holds–*

will he contain his lover

will he hold his lover's tears

will he grasp closeness

in another language

grasp & gasp of skin

Born in the year of the boar

To begin breath in the year of the boar
is to be wise, my mother tells me & later I learn,
aside from humans, pigs are the only animal
that go to the forest purposefully & get drunk.
Father tells me of Vishnu diving into the sea
to rescue Bhu Devi, Earth goddess, who creates

a world where all of us can imagine & create
new origin myths. Vishnu as a wild boar –
he has many avatars: walking across the sea,
Jesus, & Buddha also, reincarnations. I learn
some choose to incorporate, not reject, the drunk
evening taking everything in unsated: animals

squabbling behind the bins, two lovers, animal
grasp & gasp of skin, turned secrets created
in dilated eyes of sparkling girls, long drunk
on beer. Booze, the first commodity we boars
took when lockdown was announced. We learned
what society couldn't live without as the sea

thrashed against the shore, uncaring. The sea
holds its violence in check, releases an animal
breath. I count one-to-nine, then repeat. I learn
deep breathing – try stillness, try creating
it by switching off my phone. I think of boars
running free. Remember running free & drunk

that summer? I dream of holding you, drunk
on touching & closeness. Of falling to the sea
bottom & breathing deep, as Vishnu, the boar,
forages the sea floor, among forest & animal,
for what is not of ocean. My sister creates
a paper swan to float as long as paper lasts. I learn

to cry at petals falling & fallen fireflies. I learn
that letting go is nothing like the movies & the drunk
artist on the corner provides no answer as he creates
an echo of constellations. There will always be sea
rising, the cry of gulls as waves drown animals
& promises of shelter & the coarse cries of wild boars

as they create a nest for their young to learn that safety
is temporary. The boars, inebriated by the drunk
sea, drown their cubs, an animal inundation of spume.

Ghazal: ocean water

Today, spilt bucket in the kitchen. No milk, only ocean water
& satellite data, over which you sit. Salt eyes leak ocean water.

In search of salt syllables, I acquire an echo-sounder, expert in
bathymetry, find forests on the sea floor depths of ocean water.

In your eyes, only the sea's whiteness, as tendons split apart
your deck & cupped hands measure infinity in ocean water.

I am conscious of my fingertips, that rivers do meet & the sun
repeats its rise & disappearance against the edge of ocean water.

Often, I tear edges out of sandpaper. In defence of fragments,
I piece together printed seams, ink loosens, thins in ocean water.

I thin my bones to fit between the streams of your disrupted sleep.
Where you go at night is unimaginable. What part of ocean water?

In this forever night, I count colour as some count sheep. The field
is flooded & what you think is grass are watersnakes in ocean water.

I reach to touch your surface, tides ascending skin. In the morning,
cold & clouded, I find bite-marks on my fins, scars of ocean water.

From the boat window, foam lapping

at edges. You & I discuss pyrotechnics, white shattering blue.
Someone lights a fuse. Sparks like goldfish. Is this another world now
breaking into ours, slicing the night & everything bleeding out now
raw & beautiful. Come with me & collapse, our bodies burnt & new.

I want you as crabs need to scuttle over coke caps. You count labels
advertising *Evian, Mountain Valley Spring, The Genuine
Water Co.*, flasks tossed like bait, florescent cans. The urine-
coloured bags collide like jellyfish: there are no jellyfish, no Naples,

no Netherlands, no Shanghai. We have the word 'coral' & the colour,
but not the monk seal's hum finding its mate, & as calcium carbonate
dissolves & the shell of tiny shrimp disintegrates, you order dressed

prawns with crisps. This is how we went to war with ocean, lover
by lover. In search of turtles, we find only floating plastic & by it,
cigarette-butts bent like lips, & a dead penguin, ordure-caressed.

After Auden's 'Musée des Beaux Arts'

i.

Published in 1940	*something amazing*	already
Poland ravaged	& the poet walks *dully along*	Renata taken
Cecilia taken	amid all of this –	Janek
(where is Janek?)	the gypsies on the plains	annihilated & meanwhile
Auden focusses on a	painting of	*an expensive*
delicate ship	passing	*not an important failure*
the people on the shore busy	ignoring	the splash
the ploughman	not recognizing	a boy falling out
the sky	legs disappearing	feathers into foam
(where is Janek?)	reduced to	ekphrasis
the politician talks about	statistics while	reporters film drowning

The way we plough	*through life*	in 'Icarus
Again'	writes Devenish	*you'd think*
we'd have enough	*of falling*	enough of myth &
theory	particularly	Eurocentric vision
how long will Greek be	(assumed) universal	Kantaris says
the whole Aegean	*not wide enough*	*to hold the impact*
of death. Today	Icarus	is a refugee
dumped	along the journey	*because tragedies happen*
Icarus is	everything	you want her to be
a *civil war*	*slays* her, says Coleman	loose as feathers
fallen woman	made metaphor	through history

For instance, Lucrece

undone   according to convention   searching
desperate   through bejewelled hallways of   gold-spun narrative
for a means to mourn   critics scrutinising   form (ignoring
her violation)   aesthetics, internal pararhyme   the dactyl inserted
couplets   with the voyeur's gaze   making three, spectator
penetrating meaning   assimilating himself   as Tarquin
scopophilic analysis   as Art Historian, then   celebrating Titian's
naked spectacle   the titillating curtain   rude-cover coming off—
divine revelation–   breasts heaving   *beauty's wrack*
in the Fitzwilliam Museum almost stabbed   in Botticelli, already dead
Dürer paints her   in the same pose as Eve   damned, only once
daggered   destroyed, is she   mourned & loved

as long as paper lasts

In an antique land

Amitav Ghosh retraces the footsteps of a slave from the footnote
fragments of the left-behind. When the library burns & the village
burns, when the river buries our fingerprints – how many anecdotes
of wet limbs & sunsets, fat fingers in thick pies, butterflies, are pillaged
& drifting? The Geniza's sacred papers – the folklore & fairy-folk
history of Jewish-Muslim solidarity in Egypt – are translated by ship
to Cambridge, & in Cairo the stories are lost like a train in the smoke
carrying the last of our supplies. Who will tell our stories: purple lips
torn & tugged, all passion & teeth & the brittle peace of after. Crows
observe our violence. But under the painted arches of the Mosque-
converted Cathedral, my body wanting & your sour smell, dirt glow
of fingertips & candlelight, I remember the outline of your walk
outside, the fresco of Jesus, with its accompanying Koranic script,
the lilac scent & yellow willows making love again by the crypt.

Family funerals

Hanna begins: *My parents were true liberals -*
raised one radical lesbian feminist daughter,
one ultra-orthodox, Hasidic son, my brother, Saul.

Just arrived from Jerusalem's Jewish quarter,
he closes with the Kaddish, tears disrupting speech,
in my religion, real men cry, this holy water.

Hanna's partner rolls her eyes, fingers kitsch
paper flowers bunched by the bench. Dad
glances at his cousins, remembers the pitch

in NW where they'd play, the pool's lily-pads
folded at edges, unpacking their twilight
in London's rose-smoke sky, the neon ads

winking as they walk to the tube that night,
promising stars will still twinkle, if only man-
made. The crack-addicts on the Avenue cite

little reassurances. Dad's sister's there too, soon
for the last time, all dissolving into evening,
lamp seeping colour out of everything, cocooned

until every thing is sepia & swollen & clinging
to one last chance to say I love you. Later,
the dank air, salt taste of sweat & dying,

the argument over cremation or burial, blurted
words, pointed fingers. Now, a clenched peace,
as Hanna stands: *Follow Saul if you'd prefer*

a religious ceremony or me for a simple piece
of honey cake, a cup of tea. We exit as the wind
outside begins its long descent. A flock of geese

passes overhead, the birds arrowlike outlined
in red, the sun sinking spirals over each of us,
looking up at their powerful tread. Later, Dad finds

family photographs: all the kids, lips like rust,
frowning at their game of chess, then laughing,
limbs tumbling, legs entangled in the dust.

Butterfly pauses by Hanna's neck. The little things
of childhood we forget. The umber in yellow wings.

Polish honey cake

We inherit the ritual. Orange skins peeled,
we try to boil away

the bitterness, the way
my grandmother boils

hot milk, the way it overflows, the way
there's not enough

milk, and too much
skin.

*

My grandmother takes pills.
My grandmother makes me eat

each grain of rice. There is no room
for leftovers. My father says

this comes from trauma. That rice is never simply
rice. You add sugar to the boiling, this boils out

bitterness, this assimilates, softens
all kinds of things.

*

I learn to distill water. I learn to kill
bacteria. I learn

to eat my rice. Taken hot, the water
scalds, each blistered throat

is a muted scream.

*

My grandmother opts for silence.
The thing she's not got over –

what it is to live. Is this the purpose
of all those stories of survival. To make heroes

of us. To convince ourselves that living
is not some kind

of violence. Is there a reason for
indifference.

*

These things I know:
you panic in front of the police.

When they search for explosives.
When there are no explosives.

After sugar, stir in raisins
& sultanas. There is an order.

Each year we replicate
the order. I must eat

each grain of rice.

Why did we kill Jesus?

I am six & it is Christmas morning.
We go to church before we open presents –
incense still burning from my father's
meditation, Pali words mingling with ash
at Buddha's feet, carved with swastikas,
'su' means 'good', 'asti', 'it is', in Sanskit chant.

Know the Jews killed Jesus, chants
the priest on a pink December morning.
Beyond stained windows, I see swastikas
patterned in the clouds, my present
haunted. In the chapel, I dip fingers in ash,
forge sculptures of wax, while others pray & father

photographs sarcophagi. Explains father:
the New Testament reinterprets the Old, a chant
then appropriated by Rome, making ash
of other communities. In the morning
I cry, *why did we kill Jesus?* our presence
suddenly condemned. I pass a swastika

on a bathroom door. I trace the swastika
as kids discuss their trips to Auschwitz. Father
is beaten in the streets. We wake for pujas, present
open palms & petals. A Tibetan monk chants
by the thangka in the corner, as morning
rises on the Himalayas in a cloud of ash.

At grandmother's funeral, we scatter ash,
whisper of her escape from swastikas,
pretending she was Catholic, each morning
how she found safety in Jesus. Now father
describes himself *a fan of Jesus*, he chants
an origin story: in Jesus' iconography, present

are various Pagan images, which present
unstable beginnings: sometimes, out of ash
& fire, a phoenix, reincarnated. Father chants
for reincarnation, & I listen. The swastika
in tantric texts signaling the aniconic Father:
May I be free from suffering this morning.

I wake to the chant of morning –
present in blue-tit & heron call, father
in lotus, facing the ash & swastika.

'Those who view images of Nazi atrocities become witnesses to their crimes'

The problem is not that people remember through photographs, but that they remember only the photographs -Susan Sontag

i.

Who has the right to write
suffering, to frame

woman staring out without
language. The camera-gun appropriates

her voice: *photograph of a Jew
about to be shot down*

[exhibition caption]
as viewers we stand

in the place of the weapon
of destruction, our gaze

like the photographer's, identical
to the executioner's –

what counts as evidence? Passing
a shout on the corner, elbows &

hoping someone else
will intervene, later

putting it in a poem –
that someone does

intervene or the argument
is resolved, a misunderstanding,

a one-off. Say
you photographed

the sunset & what looks like
two lovers

elbows & hoping –
are we reliable as witnesses?

ii.

Two statues:

one little girl & boy, behind them
another little girl & boy of iron-cast

aside two sides, a boundary line
one commemorates children

fleeing to safety via kinder-transport, the other
kids killed in the camps –

statues made for collective
recollection, Berlin united

in the memory
of what happened last time

Germany was ruled from Berlin. Tragedy
manipulated to create

togetherness. What is remembered
at Auschwitz? The killing process

or the attempted destruction of evidence
by the Germans, an acknowledgement

of guilt. The Berlin Memorial
to the Murdered Jews, a final solution

to Germany's memory problem.
The company that produced the columns' finish

produced the gas that finished
little girls and boys. In Paris, my father

searches for sisters and brothers
in Moses baskets, at the cobbler's shop,

behind the bins of cafes,
where the hungry dart of eyes

will recognize another
with wings as arms.

iii.

In Mexico City's museum for Memoria & Tolerancia, a wall of euphemism:

Sonderbehandlung (translation) 'trato especial'
(signifies) 'killed on arrival' *Arbeit Macht Frei*

(translation) 'el trabajo libera' (signifies) 'city of ghosts'
Selektion determines 'who lives & who dies', substituting

record of genocide in Mexico –

one room on Darfur: 'el gobierno ha asesinado'
assassinated, later 'violado...

las comunidades indigenas'
in Guatemala, *violated,* in Mexico there is nothing

on the [   ] massacre,
the genocide of [   ],

but we who know remember

& when they cut our tongues

slice open our tympanic membrane

we still will seek
blue limbs, bathe skin for burial

we still will dream

the lake where flamingoes
scatter, the coral caress

of summer, how
the knowing glance of the beloved speaks

of this oyster world,
of eyes brimming water

& rainfall sweet.

In search of an archive

By the bank the Vistula River, searching for ghosts,
my brother & I in our bunk, bearing witness
to what survives: the silver birch, the last bumblebee,

the coral fish that flit & fall, caught along the coast,
crushed snails. We follow slime trails, guess
by the bank of the Vistula River, searching for ghosts

& you; but the indifferent moon reveals a host
of nothings & nowhere destinations. No promises
to what survives. The silver birch, the last bumblebee.

Will there be flowers enough for it to pollinate? Most
fade with the weight of so much suppressed
by the bank of the Vistula River. We search for ghosts:

can you hear us? Cecilia tied to the lamppost
outside the Gestapo's, Janek on his knees, baring his chest
to what survives: the silver birch, the last bumblebee,

the fallen pollen, the bitter ash. We tell our stories, boast
because stories are what we have to imagine other endings
by the bank of the Vistula River, searching for ghosts
& what survives: the silver birch, the last bumblebee.

echo of constellations

Brushstrokes

so beautiful
in the Louvre
the letter in her
destroyed
his loved ones
Ryszard
Bruno
Paris is
to seek asylum
PTSD
Cecilia
taken
wanted her
spilled blood
my grandfather
in Belzec
in Belzec
he sees her
along the Seine
imagining
finds his own
& paints her
seeks
suffering
plans
& ends up
as he looks
a statement that
it might be

in brushstrokes
my grandfather's
hands
ordered to the front line in order

in the Louvre again
at this painting of someone
there is love still
worth it

Bathsheba
loss frames
her beloved
to die
also
on the train
buying bread
a lonely place
at every corner
memory of
Cecilia again
King David
& so
later
learns she dies
what they did to her
here in Paris
in every face
as Rembrandt
Bathsheba
beloved
as my grandfather
an end to
each day
the final day
tears spilling
so loved
& perhaps
to stay alive

Reflections of the bumblebee (iii)

As monks,
black-hooded

antennae
bowed, we

mourn
green sphynx

moth & tiger
beetle –

they too have
lost their

nesting –
remember

us & stone
grasshoppers in

buttercup
meadows

at least
there are still

buttercups
if only

buttercups.

The night does not discriminate

Empty hotels in Tel Aviv are overrun by wild boars,
their snouts scuffling the last of days, tusks piercing
the April sky. I skype you in the middle of the night.
Again, we discuss how pigs get drunk, seeking
fermented apples in hawthorn woods. How we share
98% of our DNA. When lockdown was announced,

I bought wine, then rice. The government announced
increases in alcohol consumption, empty shelves. I bore
through hours, more cheap Rioja, Heineken cans. Share
memes, obsess over tweets & cleaning products. Pierce
my earlobes. Rearrange my Pink Floyd CDs. Seek
to shift the dust monotony of days, count sirens in the night.

Can you hear the birds? Swallows shedding sleep as night
fades to laburnum & cherry blossom. You announce
today is the first day of Ramadan & together, we seek
out sacred myths. How Meleager hunts the giant boar,
Jibril's revelation to Mohammad, the angel's piercing
gaze, a promise of mossy ground for us all to share.

You say this virus is punishment for our not sharing,
our always taking & wanting & wanting, but the night
does not discriminate or know pandemic. The stars pierce
equally the moth & butterfly, the nurse who announces
I cannot save your father & *I'm so sorry*, the boars
that leave behind their hungry young while they seek

food. Outside, green flourishing, another spring seeking
breath. I wish I could kiss you. Instead, reckless sharing
of false information, callousness. You explain, the boar
saves Osiris, guards Freyr, his sister Freyja, like the night
which won't discriminate & in the purple we announce
a commitment to find a way through difference. To pierce

the pernicious opinions we have of one another. Pierce
this distance & risk the price of tenderness. I seek
it like a firefly to sunlight, as petals bloom announcing
the possibility of something more – perhaps the sharing
of clean water, of flower-scented air, knowing the night
which won't discriminate will protect the wild boar,

the nest. It will announce the footfall of hunter, pierce
danger. We will seek softness & nuzzling & the boar
will watch rain share its wetness, the small palms of night.

Love song for the tightrope walkers

For they rebuild the nests of starling & hummingbird, feed
the wolf-cub who's lost its mother, afraid of its own shadow,
for they too are considered less important when the wind blows
unwelcome, stocking supermarket shelves, before agreed

shifts in cabaret bars. Sammy balances on one hand & strips,
takes back tips to his boyfriend, saves some for the sequin girl
with the ill grandpa who's short on rent. Each night, she unfurls
her wings, falls & flies, transforms this audience of sceptics

& unbelievers. Do you hear the white river rush from the source,
the shuffling cry of morning? I have seen the coral snake outrun
its skin, the mangrove soak up the swamp, the ceiba roots retake

each brick & bone the Mayans leave behind. They'll chart a course
to sunlight, from maize-leaf to lily-pad, when you & I have gone
to dark; & in that faded starlight, jacaranda spirits wake.

I cannot promise you an eternity

of love, you sing to me
the last time I see you.

      You are mostly

tubes & purple
veins. You write

      & I hold steady

your frail fingers clutching
the pen. Tell me again

      of your arrival

in Mexico in 1935,
of whom you left behind. I ask,

      does it bother you

to be blind. I am stupid
& seven years old.

      You are concerned

by the disappearance
of butterflies. I lose

      the paper message you

write, I think
on the 12 hour flight

back, but I can't be sure.

I admit this to my mum
on my 24th birthday. *Búscalo,*

maybe it will turn up

somewhere. Someone writes
all lost things end up

on the moon. Tell me

about the prison
in Germany. Tell me

so I can record

the name you shed
so the others wouldn't

find you. My friend

holds a full-moon
ritual in which we burn

what we wish to forget.

You receive a death threat
on a Tuesday afternoon. *Put it*

in the third drawer down

with all the others,
you say. In the last days

you speak only German.

None of us understand.
In Mexico City, I find

someone to translate

the words you mumble
in sleep, *are there*

enough butterflies

in all the world
for all the flowers?

Notes

The epigraph, by Marianne Frenk is from her book *Mariposa, Eternidad de lo Efímero* (1982). It can be translated as 'I do not promise you eternal love, but is not each moment in love its own eternity?'. The title of my closing poem *I cannot promise you an eternity* makes reference to this epigraph.

In the morning: Coyoacan is a district in Mexico City.

On finding the painted walls of Bonampak: Bonampak is a Mayan archeological site in the Lacandona jungle in Chiapas.

Elegy to the Howler Monkeys: Fanny Hill refers to the protagonist of John Cleland's *Memoirs of a Woman of Pleasure* (1748). Berger references John Berger's *Ways of Seeing* (1972).

Return: Chichen Itzá is a Mayan archeological site in Yucatan. La Malinche is the Spanish name for the indigenous translator of Cortés.

The Roman Sarcophagus is all that's left: in the footnotes, the following words are in Spanish: 'turistas' meaning 'tourists'; 'todas operadas', 'all operated'; 'la revolución feminista', 'the feminist revolution'. Limpia is a spiritual purification ritual. The Mexican Barbasco trade involved the pilfering of the Lacandona jungle for the Barbasco plant, traditionally used by indigenous communities, and selling it to pharmaceutical companies to make synthetic hormones. In the process of manufacturing safe contraceptives for American populations, many unsafe drugs were trialed outside the US, with devastating results.

Transnational zoo: In 'Hide', the line 'in what language rain falls over tormented cities' is borrowed from Neruda's El libro de las preguntas.

In *Prey*, Xolotl is the Aztec dog-headed god of lightening and fire, and the guide of dead souls to the underworld. 'Calzada de Tlalpan', 'Juarez', 'General Anaya' and 'Francisco Sosa' are roads in Mexico City.

In *Cage*, the following words are in Yucatec Maya, spoken by the Maya people of the Yucatec peninsula: 'Kan' is 'Snake'; 'Chakmool' is 'Jaguar'; 'Chuwen' is 'Monkey'; 'Aak' is 'Turtle'; 'Aayin' is 'Alligator'. The following words are in Nahuatl, the language of the Aztecs and of the Nahua people of central Mexico: 'Chapulin' is 'Grasshopper'; 'Quetzal' is the name for a Mesoamerican bird. For the Maya people living in the Lacandona jungle in Chiapas: Akyantho' is the god of foreigners, responsible for trade and disease; the god Tuub is the son of the god Hachakyum, who created the jungle; the god Kisin is responsible for death and earthquakes. Since evangelical missionaries from the US arrived in the Lacandona jungle, among which was the Summer Institute, some Lacandona communities have accepted Jesus Christ as the son of Akyantho'.

Christmas in diaspora: 'Babcia', is the Polish word for 'grandmother'. The Pali chant, 'nammo ta sa bhagavato arahato samma', is a homage to the Buddha in the Theravada Buddhist tradition.

On not-translating Neruda: the epigraph quotes the 2001 edition and translation by William O'Daly of Pablo Neruda's The Book of Questions, published by Copper Canyon Press. In the poem, 'es verdad' means both 'it is true' and 'is it true' in Spanish, depending on intonation; 'contigo en una noche estrellada' means 'with you in a starry ['estrellada' also means 'stretched out' or 'shattered'] night'; 'contigo hasta la luz del dia se suicida' means 'with you until the light of day kills itself [or commits suicide]'; 'bajo una ola morada, enamorada' means 'underneath a purple wave, in love'. The line 'contigo en una noche estrellada' is a nod to Neruda's 'la noche está estrellada' in his 'Poema 20' (1924).

After Auden's Musée des Beaux Arts: (i) borrows the lines indicated in italics from W. H. Auden's 'Musée des Beaux Arts' (1940). (ii) borrows the following lines: 'the way we plough through life' and 'you'd think we'd have enough of falling' from Alan Devenish's 'Icarus Again' (1999); 'the whole Aegean not wide enough to hold the impact' from Sylvia Kantaris' 'Some Untidy Spot' (1989); and 'civil war slays' from Wanda Colemen's 'In Search of the Mythology of Do Wah Wah' (1983).

For instance, Lucrece: the italicized line is from Shakespeare's *The Rape of Lucrece* (1594).

In an antique land: the title references the 1992 book written by Amitav Ghosh.

Family Funerals: the Kaddish is a hymn of praises about God found in Jewish mourning services.

Those who view Nazi atrocities become witnesses to their crimes: the title comes 'from Janet Jacobs, Memorialising the Holocaust: Gender, Genocide and Collective Memory (2010); the epigraph is from Susan Sontag's Regarding the Pain of Others (2003). In (iii) I provide false translations of the Spanish 'trato especial', which should translate as 'special treatment', and 'el trabajo libera', which should translate as 'work sets you free'.

I cannot promise you an eternity: the Spanish imperative 'búsaclo' means 'look for it'. The lines 'are there/enough butterflies/in all the world/for all the flowers' are my translations of lines from Marianne Frenk's book, Mariposa, Eternidad de lo Efímero (1982).